Horridge

To Cambo
Ith ∩ love
Hugh
25/1/95

Horridge

Hugh McMillan

Chapman Publishing
1994

Published by
Chapman
4 Broughton Place
Edinburgh EH1 3RX
Scotland

A catalogue record for this volume is
available from the British Library.
ISBN 0-906772-52-4

Chapman New Writing Series
Editor Joy Hendry
ISSN 0953-5306

Some of these poems have previously appeared in

The Scotsman, Scotland on Sunday, Chapman, Northlight, Northwords,
Cencrastus, Poetry Review, New Writing Scotland, Krino, Cyphers,
Gairfish, The Limerick Poetry Broadsheet, Spectrum, Rebel Inc and the
postcard set *Horridge,* Hugh Who, Dumfries 1992.

Designed & typeset by Peter Cudmore
Cover Design by Fred Crayk

Printed by
Mayfair Printers
Print House
William Street
Sunderland
Tyne and Wear

Contents

Contents

Foreword

It's a singular honour to preface this distinguished collection by Hugh McMillan not least because I only met the poet once, when fishing him out of a canal in Galway City into which he had tumbled after a brief, though not uneventful, meeting with Ciaran Hanlan, Ireland's self-proclaimed "Bard of Poteen". In a way I feel better qualified to discuss his performance as a swimmer which I have to say on the day was lamentable, sinking being a more apposite description. Nor am I myself a great and authoritative figure in the literary scene. In fact I was passing the canal on my bicycle with a sultana cake when I first encountered serious writing, in the shape of the incident described above. I believe Hugh McMillan has himself given a highly stylised account of this event in one of those Scottish literary magazines that appear sporadically and I would be grateful for a photocopy of this because I'm sure the poet has underplayed my own role in the affair while exalting his own into some kind of metaphysical triumph. Suffice it to say that were it not for me this collection would be a posthumous one, though perhaps it would be none the worse for that.

After meeting the poet in such circumstances I have, of course, followed his career with interest and with a growing and heavy sense of guilt, for in the eyes of posterity will I not be judged at least partly responsible for what he has produced since? This is not a comfortable responsibility. Old ladies mortally offended by his verse look to me for explanations which I am unable to provide. Why does the man not concentrate on seagulls? they ask. He has proved himself a master with such birds in the past, as well as trees which nearly always, as the man is perniciously depressed, are "naked and shivering" and clouds which, because he writes in Dumfries, a liability few critics have chosen to take into account, are nearly always "rags". Sometimes the seagulls are "rags" too, which admittedly is confusing but at least it is poetry. Unhappily, however, when Hugh McMillan writes about Scotland he often resorts to a type of language that my Great Aunt Mary used to say "grows from the gutter", though I suppose to his credit the nature of the country encourages this kind of response in its poets, or Machars, as they call them.

I have subscribed to many Scottish journals and magazines and occasionally these contain famously small doses of the work of Hugh McMillan. I have also scanned many anthologies of verse hoping to find his name in respectable company but in this I have failed. He was not in the *20 Best Scottish Poets* anthology, the *20 More of the Same* anthology, or the *32 Poets Who Live In The Central Belt Not In Any Anthology Yet* anthology. I am saddened to see that he has not even been included in the recently published *Best of Young Bald Scottish Poets* anthology. Saddened but not surprised. He is as bald as a billiard ball under that wig but, frankly, the man is not young. He is 65 at least, though he apes the appearance and manners of a Bohemian. As for whether he's a poet or not, I have to leave that to you.

Fintan O'Halloran
Galway City, 25 January 1994

The World Book of the McMillans ⸋

Dear **Hugh McMillan**,
you have been selected by our clan computer
to receive a copy of
**The World Book of the McMillans $149.95
(including unique hand painted coat of arms)**.
Have you ever considered, **Hugh McMillan**,
your family ties and heritage?
In these pages, **Hugh**,
you will bear witness to the heroism
and industriousness of your ancestors
and learn about the forbears
who shaped the history of the world,
like **Fergus McMillan, the 8th Man of Moidart,
Hector 'Steamboats' McMillan,
the inventor of the 12 Bore Scrotal Pump Beam,
Brian 'Big Shuggie' McMillan, Golf Caddie to the Stars**,
and many many others,
though probably not **Archie McMillan**
who died of silicosis
or **James and Colin** who drowned in the Minch,
or **Struan** who drank himself to death
in that corner of the Central Bar.
To bear witness to that kind of thing,
Hugh McMillan,
it costs a bit more.

Bright Blue

Politics in the back room
of Billy Bridges Bar.
The wind is howling through the roofs of Ayr,
loosening more slates.
Workmen on ladders struggle to impose Christmas
on the brown backcloth of the day.
"We'd have nae SAY,
we'd be like one o they tin pot places,
Italy or Spain".
They shake their dominoes,
cast them on the table like bones.
Nae Say, agree the doms grimly.
We struggle deeper in our cardigans
which are all brown as beer,
beneath the poster of the Highland cow
stoned by nicotine,
a coat of arms, crossed half pints
on an ash field,
The Glenfinnan Monument keeking
from a ring of smoke.
The whole room is decorated
by that firm that specialises in paint
to suit the Scottish psyche:
Dulux's Potato Brown
or Shades of a Shitey Sunday Night.
Brown.
Brown as mince and teapots,
brown as anoraks,
brown as smoked sausage suppers,
brown as the sky staggering over
to Ireland across the clapped out sea,

brown as the flag hanging drowned
above the Forum Arcade,
Ayr's Brownest Shopping Experience.
Good job we don't live in Spain.
With all that sharpness
we might have to stretch to definitions,
tell dark from light,
day from night,
burn our cardies,
chuck away our doms,
FIND ANOTHER COLOUR.

The Oban Experience

Heritage Wharf.
The Tourists are queuing
for a sniff at Oban Station, 1900,
the walls in studied sepia,
the prints of cheery railway barons,
the sights, the smells, the mystery...

The mystery is why anyone
should use this kind of voodoo
to invoke a past that never was
while outside, thirty feet outside,
beyond the thin fringe of mastheads,
the sea bends away to rub the skulls of islands,
a phrenology of history,
not a hologram or clockwork gull in sight

just a sad story worth divining.

West Coast

Midnight,
and the moon focuses like a projectionist,
reveals segment shows
of salt-blocked buildings and gulls,
a bulbfield of gulls, watching.
We divine their pragmatism
in the entrails of net,
in the abandoned hive of creels.

Earlier that day
we had watched a drunken man
put the French to flight.
"I'm a Scottish fisherman", he was shouting,
"Who the fuck are you?"
They pedalled off, all smiles,
correctly guessed it was a historical tableau.

Midnight.
At our hands, clapping,
the gulls explode like fragments
of the same eternal gull,

until there's only one in view,
a rag flapping over the bay,
like a tease.

Home Brew

Inverbervie, Stonehaven, Port Lethen,
like an incantation to the beat of engines,
the bus is coursing through Scotland's jugular,

each name,
each cottage at the ankles of hills,
each field broken by frost,
part of a broth

into which whirl
toothless men at five-bar gates,
wee boys on dykes,
bungalows perched like pith helmets,
boats, rigs, cows, keeps.

It's the end of another year,
bubbling to a close in the ink
of the Moray Firth.

I stand on a cliff while the sea
tries to define the coast
and the sky grumbles overhead
like the lid on a kettle.

Some Scottish Problems Resolved

1. The Mystery of Pictish Symbol Stones and the origins of the Saltire. (Some people say that the Saltire was adopted as the flag of Scotland when Oengus, King of the Picts, saw the cross of St Andrew displayed miraculously across the sky above his victorious army.)

Retainer of King Oengus:

>Fuck me, will ye look at that.
>Ah hevnie seen an arrangement like
>that since we spotted the wan that looked
>like a zebra on a surfboard –
>ye ken, the thing we carve on aa the stanes.

King Oengus himself:

>Christ, yer right.
>Come an we'll adopt it as our national motif.
>It'll be easier to scratch on wa's
>an a fucking sight less confusing
>for ethnologists.

A Scottish Hoy-You

(A Hoy-You is an ancient Scottish verse form of 3 lines
and 15 syllables, traditionally written by people who have
nothing to say and addressed to those who don't want to
hear it. The 1990s seem a particularly favourable context
in which to reinvent this classical form.)

> Here's tae us, wha's
> like us? Dam few an they're aa
> on tea towels.

Tam Rejects the Consolation
of the Church

Okay, Christ suffered,
but only for three days,
and he didn't have to.
I know God gave his son for us
but it was the kind of death
a properly-motivated man
might manage for a cause.

What kind of following would he have had
if God had reserved for his son
the kind of death that ordinary folk have to suffer,
some lingering terminal disease
where you can just drag yourself around
and no more, your guts and soul rotted away.

He had a crisis of faith
after a few hours.
My mother was eaten away for 360 days,
and not alone;
the rest of us bled to a kind of death
that made dangling on a piece of wood
look a dawdle.

I don't think he died for us:
I know he didn't die like us.

Old Bobby Spoils a Night Out

"You've got to give it to them,
though you hate the bastards."
We are talking about Glasgow Rangers,
when Bobby, an old man
whose face has imploded round a Monty moustache
and a mouth liberated from teeth,
sits between us.
He is shouting
but not in a language that needs words,
though I believe it is about the war,
and he is wearing the Africa Star.

We ignore him,
"They were lucky in the first half, though..."
 but Bobby is up, shadow wrestling.
He has these plastic slip-on shoes
and a sockless white ankle
protruding like a bone.
He's prodding it at our feet,
getting leverage,
tugging at something with his arms,
poking it, twisting it,
his mouth filling with spit.

"They did well, you have to say it"
You have to say it
or see that brown blood in the sun
or his hand about to turn your face to his.
"What the fuck does he want? Absolution?
Another Medal?"
It's in his eyes what he wants,
·it's in his eyes
like ice.
They did well the boys,
you have to say,
you have to.

Solway Unit on the Beach

They stood strung out on the shore,
far off, like white wood
driven in at the line of tide.
Through gaps, even, it seemed

through parchment skin ran
tongues of sky
and the gun-metal sea. Inside
our shoulders shook

and we roared
with laughter at the sight
of that mad crew filed
along the empty beach.

Someone called them in
(We couldn't bear to leave
the beery warmth and go outside)
but they didn't hear or anyway stayed

rooted along the edge. Close to,
their eyes bored through me, mirroring the void,
and their arms stretched wide
to catch the bitter breeze.

Soor Faced Sue

Sue was at her worst with men.
When a new boy came onto the ward
you would get him to say hello to Sue
then stand back and watch the fun.
Hello, she'd murmur, then smile,
and lunge with blunt fingers at his eyes.
The Ashludie Kiss, we'd call it.

She was a mad one,
but when she cried for her Ma
in the middle of the night
you'd swear it was a wee girl
and sometimes, like when
she had that Minister by the chukkies,
shouting You fucking smarmy wee bald bastard,
she seemed the height of reason.

A Very Straight Line [x]

In the parlour of the pub
the squirrel looped the same loop,
the morse of its belly
spelling out a monotonous distress,
front paws flip,
back paws down,
then blink,
at the same vista,
the blurred threat of a falcon
stuffed and primed,
the tatty drapes,
the light through brown bottled glass.

One day,
and I swear it was tó spring me, not him,
I unhooked the cage.
He paused,
spun backwards,
and sped out the door
in one straight line,
and when he should have sensed the wheels
he didn't swerve
as if this trajectory
was what he'd dreamed of,
all our circular days.

The Black Gulls

Dumfries, the Old Bridge,
a thumbnail past seven,
the sun squeezing past confident clouds.
Lean over and see
hidden trees on the surface
moving without wind
and walls swimming
and gulls racing their blunt images
across the silence,
through the towers of the town
dreamily shaking,
and there, my head,
set square in the hieroglyph of reed and water,
in place.
How long passes?
There are homes and pubs
and people waiting
but the black gulls, their flight is perfect,
matching dip and dart and distance
and never leaving
the rapture of the dark.

Riding at the Moon

Through cataracts of dust
I see Kirkconnel fading,
shadow welling through trees,
spreading a tidemark on the hills like oil.
The train has stopped, a cold witness
to dark closing like a fist over the silent town
and its streets, swept by soft and insistent rain,
pattering like hoofs.

This stop is not timetabled.
There are no passengers
on an abstract journey into night,
no people at all in the train,
or outside in the rain,
though in the last of the light
I seem to see a straight-backed girl
riding at the pieces of the moon.

Impressions

St Andrews,
the wind tearing at the sky,
brown corners of cloud flapping,
gulls tumbling across wells of blue
cut like iceholes
and freezing over.
The wet sand is like glass.
You turn back with your camera,
back towards the outcrop of town,
crouch down.
The wind lifts your hair,
lets it fall.
In the distance a horse
at the rim of the sea
barely twitches.

No photograph, you shrug,
I don't take photographs any more.
You give a little smile,
and the horse circles and charges,
circles, charges,
and we walk back,
leaving no footprints
on the sand.

Sundown

It is nearly night,
the sun is calling home the light
through minarets of metal and wire,
through hills quietly sleeping,
through street lamps blinking
in the dips of distance,
through regiments of trees
dragging their heels
and seagulls nagging
at the scorched hems of fields.

Opposite, in the melt
of the train's neon
and a last sunlight
pale as a pearl above the beard of cloud,
another beloved landscape.
Hair like embers, head unbowed,
who will call you to sleep?
Only I will see that miracle;
the darkening of that star.

At the Swings

Puddles,
and bracelets of scuffed bloom.
The wet trees butt water
and the river noses past the bridge,
the arches stubbled with moss,
to where reeds swim with sandstone
in a black mirage
and only the punctuation of swans,
bent like question marks,
dazzle.

He swings,
his bright red shoes a challenge
to the consensus of cloud and rooftiles,
the wash of grey and green.
He stretches out his hands,
palm outwards,
"I can let go, and hold onto nothing."

He's kept me moored like a full stop
on this page
that he'll desert one day
without a thought.
There's colour in the world,
a dazzle of colour,
but where could I go to see
such a brush stroke,
bold against the sky?
I could let go,
but I would hold onto nothing.

Play

We sit, my son and I,
on the train from Larbert,
playing with our toys.
He has Bret the Hit Man Hart
and I have a new can of Export,
bright as a pillar box.
Haaaaaaa he whispers, haaaaaaaa,
it is the noise of a crowd in his head.
It has a large capacity, his head,
all seated like Ibrox Park.
I myself am waiting for the plastic tag
that bears the letter X.
It is on the bottom of the can
and will win us a holiday in Barbados
at the Liver Unit of my choice.
While we play, Scotland flicks unnoticed by,
its fins of frost, trees cupping cold hands,
living rooms stiff with Sunday,
then we bounce into Glasgow.
"Still time" he says, "still time"
and Bret lunges for a clothes line
or is it a folding body press? I don't know,
I am watching foam recede from
a smooth and endless shore.
No X, only a blurred reflection
of a place, a person, I should be.

Surprise Attacks

I hear the sound of a boy
waiting to be ambushed
by his father,
that carpet of smells and roars
like a bear, all hugs and stubble.
Each step breaks on the stairs like ice
and it precedes him, this excitement,
like a shadow mad and off its moorings.
Oh, should we not weep
for the ghosts of undiluted joy
and the years I cannot wish for him
but he is eager, all fists, for.

It is a long minute.
He is stopped, poised on one leg
like a crane.
Perhaps he will be a dancer
or a poet
it doesn't matter.
Whether he requires it for his art or not
he will be ambushed by his father,
from the tops of trees
the tips of pencils
the precipitation of sleep
he will be ambushed by his father,
when he is old and threadbare
and sick of such surprises,
even then
he will be ambushed by his father.

Turning

Mist. A blurring.
The hedges and streets
– it's more than a disguise –
are off centre,
under new management.
There is change, a stiffening,
like some premonition of death,
lovely and grave.

I see my son sleeping,
one minute sucking that old T-shirt,
the moon full on his face,
the next kicking long legs at the blanket,
his mouth rehearsing,
slowly, in this season of course,
turning.

Tea Leaves

There's a grey poignancy in this weather,
these October afternoons
disguised as night.
The cafe's empty,
stare out the window.

There's a boy with scarlet cheeks
beside a skinny tree,
pockets swollen with treasure.
He throws the leaves
and catches them in his hair

and he is thinking of Swan's
and the dark shelves of comics
never dreaming – any more than old Swan
with his bursting bank account and blood vessels –
of prophecies in the settling rags of brown
though they were plain as tea leaves.

The Fire and the Flowers

We slow down
and the sun bounds down the train.
In a field below the embankment,
an angle of light and flowers,
there are two boys.
One is lining up a penalty,
the other, a year or so smaller,
is swaying, ready for the save.
Overhead the clouds are high,
fragmented, like string.

We inch past
as the boy runs up.
A breeze sets the white flowers off
like applause.
I add larch trees to the scene
in a long fringe to the left,
some houses behind.
I press my face against the glass
and see the kick,
head-high to the goalie's right,
a great shot.
I see him leap, his hand curve,
I see it and the ball blaze
in the white of the sun.

Then they're gone.
There's no save, no goal,
only the beat of the train
and the countdown to Kilmarnock,
only deadly logic to suggest
the end to such dynamics.

The Window

Open upwards,
scorns gardens cowed by fuchsia,
hosepipes, cars parked too perfectly,
the cramped sounds and sizzles
of tea-time in Dumfries,
the bleeps, the woofs, the tinny tunes,
the children crying.

It is an invitation for clouds
to peek like schoolkids and run away,
for sudden sunlight and a rhythm-line of rain,
for breeze to gently take the piss

and sometimes at night
it opens up
as if all the stars had to look at was us,
and only the gossip of leaves
reminds us that there are other points of view.

In the Frame

Staring at that slice of blue cloud
and the sun hung like an onion
between half-lengths of lamppost
and the strange stalks of buildings.

There is a maniac muttering in my ear,
the way maniacs in toilets do,
some homily about piss
or hurrying back for beer.

But it is better here,
where you can't see the doorsteps
that daily clamp this sandwich in place,
where for a moment you can escape the frame

and there seem such possibilities
for you and I
in the arrangements of clouds and sky
and the distant base of engines

from a road I could draw just there
in that gap between the window and the Xpelair,
draw it between the hems of stone and briar
like a crowbar.

A Wee Word ˣ

Dear Sir, a member of the School Board –
who must remain faceless –
saw you cuddling Miss Dewar
outside the Dumfries Arms last night.
He was passing in a fast car
and wasn't really looking
but saw you stroking her hair
and nuzzling that little diamond of neck
with your nose,
and you a married man.

Given such examples
our pupils may no longer be content
to conjugate, to add or subtract,
to think decently in French.
They might conclude that loving
dark-haired girls in public is a good idea;
that it's possible for a grown man
to be weak, or wrong, or dreaming still.

Where would all this end?
It would no longer be safe to walk
the streets after Badminton.
We would no longer be secure
in our bungalows,
worse,
in our pronouncements.

Readings of October

Once more, October,
with its squalls
and secretive moon.
I'm staring at these walls,
the orange flowers, the damp,
the dunts, the dud starts.
How could anyone sit in this room
and not see it unroll from right to left,
a personal makimono?
Because it is dead,
beyond decoding.
Upstairs, asleep, a new literature
is born from these scraps
but on my horizon
there is only a red balloon
lashed to a clothes line
furiously signalling,
dipping at the mud
then straining for a glimpse
up the cuffs of cloud.

Brooms Road

On Brooms Road it is raining,
traffic is snuffling along the street
and the sky is wrinkled
like velvet.

In the back room I find the boy
blowing bubbles that bounce down
towards the trees that used to skin
my knees. It is bright sunlight.

"It's on top, the weather" he says.
Bubbles blow back, drift and disappear.
Some burst but certainly not all.
Rain is still in my ears

but I see his head and the hills
and it is clear now
which side of the house
I will live in.

Turning Taps

It is Tuesday, cold,
the last clouds are cardboard,
the moon a carved hole in ice.
I walk down this street with its red brick,
its certainties sandwiched in sandstone
and it's hard to think of denouements,
but for once it's clear;
there is ritualism,
I have to turn the taps.

We sit, drink tea.
Dumfries kneels down to darkness
and it is difficult to see your face,
its sad beauty.
Things unsaid, said too often,
turn in the air like glass.
I've been with you too long,
too little, you say,
though it's the same.

Pinch-faced I go to drain the taps,
and free another house
of magic.

Letter from the 24th Congress of the Communist Party

(inspired by photographs of the event)

Dear Joe,
Sorry you couldn't be here,
you really missed yourself.
Krupskaya brought a quiche
but the fun really started when Bukharin
told the joke about the dyslexic deviant functionalists
and when Felix Dzerhinsky got his cock out,
turned his pockets inside out
and pretended to be Babar,
I thought I'd die.
Who said the inevitable victory of the Proletariat
was bound to be joyless?
Love Vlad.

Dr Gallagher, I presume

He is crumpled in tropical fawn;
dressed for a safari.
He sits in Ruby's,
besieged in a kraal of black-ribbed chairs
by winking bandits,
blow-piped music,
by the lustrous and budding thighs of girls.

They are trying to blow his head off with heavy metal
but he will not shift.
As an anthropologist, he has danced to beats.
"John Lennon", he muses,
"that takes me back a few wives."

Like a river, life buffets the door.
We hear parakeets screaming
from distant bungalows
and the drum of rain on cobble stone.
"*Une autre fois?*" he asks,
and when he taps the glass
it gleams like a diamond in the dark.

Hand Axe

It sits near a brochure for Gîtes,
near a plate of toast,
a percolator angrily muttering
and a child in a corner
with a cube of light,
beeping.

I found it this morning,
prised it from the kiss of clay,
saw the thick grooves for fingers,
felt the balance, perfect in my palm.
Was this the bark-splitter,
the stone-breaker?

At last
in this passing wizardry,
silence,
strength,
power.

Presences

Wee Ronnie, sunk in his parka,
moonwalking down Clarinda Drive,
holding shoulder-high a shelf he's found on a bin,
with the storm pulling at it,
blowing him down.

Jerome, in the Monastery at Cernica,
on the black walls,
hammering the plank of wood
he's holding shoulder-high,
calling God down through rings of cloud.

Is he there,
in the swirl and the trees' bleeding leaves?
The Monks file in, turn scrubbed faces to the door,
and Ronnie, on his feet for a third time,
turns round to face the gale.

Tour 4150

A metallic voice in the heat
and heavy throb of engines:
"Behind that wood is Belsen,
the German Camp."

The Courier waves sleepily
and a few necks crane,
cameras twitch, and are still.
They halt by wet trees,
by miles of black ploughed earth.

"Good to stretch your legs" they say,
and patrol the side of the road,
anxious for the bus to open again
like a womb.

A few rattle the branches,
wrinkle their noses,
but what they smell is burnt toast
in the Rasthaus,
not History.

Rejoice, there is a Jugglers' Shop

Rejoice,
there is a Jugglers' Shop
that sells padded balls and flasks,
kites and yo-yos.
Before I saw it,
horrors were in my head,
Tuzla, Nova Bila,
battles for dignity and life itself,
but we can relax,
there is a Jugglers' Shop
where the concerned can gather
to discuss juggling,
the cost of nocks and ferrules,
the effects of the SB-2,
the yo-yo NASA recommends.
Don't you know that the yo-yo
reminds us of the spinning miracle of life,
it connects us with that inner space
within us all which is always
spinning and dancing?
No?
Then rejoice,
there is a Jugglers' Shop.

History

The last whaler lives
in a cottage with black sills
sunk like a bad tooth in Henry Street.
The other houses gleam in a practiced smile
that brings tourists to one side,
and artists to a salon on the other.
The street no longer stinks of blood
but peppermint.

The whaler has a wicker chair
and a bottle of beer
stashed below.
Fuck youse, he shouts at the trippers,
at the bohemians fleeing with their paints,
fuck youse all
and he grins the wet width of his gums.

In the craftshop
among the pictures of local characters
there are no entries
for the year our man was born,
on the beach, they say,
in the shape of a dog.
After all, is it the kind of thing
you want to hear on your holiday,
a pensioner urging you to abandon
the Museum of Automata,
to go instead and fuck yourself?

They are waiting, waiting,
for an incident serious enough
to have him removed,
strangled in his bed by a hit-man
from the National Trust
and replaced, no fuss,
with a hologram or a polystyrene head
that says

Hello Boys and Girls
come in and see my life:
it was hard but we had fringe religions
and folk music,
peppermint and little crosses made from jet,
some of which are on sale inside
for as little as three quid,
for history surely

a small price to pay.

Ideal Homes

You keep the Subaru,
compact as yourself,
white as your knuckles on the wheel,
snouting north over the Corinth Canal,
over the bleached bones of Greece,
through mountains alight.
I look into your eyes,
beyond the reflection of that farm truck
with brake problems.

Three days ago, in the Cyclades,
a huge sun sank on cue
and a breeze carrying all the hot bubble
of the Peloponnese fanned my cheek
and I thought yes, yes, this is the place
but now I look into your eyes
I see a darker climate,
and I am more disposed to live there,
with all its squalls.

The Moon Over Constanza

The moon over Constanza
looks like a hole drilled in space by a genius
but Captain Fluoriu is earthbound
and as water – or oil – or aviation fuel –
drips from the roof of the Boeing onto my salami
and the man who looks like Francis Coppola
weeps gently into his half-filled beaker of wine
I keep my eyes pinned on the moon above Constanza,
even after it is sliced in two by a wingtip
and on our backs,
even after the plane has slewed to a halt
beside a walnut tree and a dog
searching in a universe of fleas,
even after that.

Small Change

Monday afternoon.
Stones like glass
and branches stirring in a tide of sky.
The road winds between poplars
into the mouth of the sun.

When the wind blows
light breaks against the cypresses
and there is fire and marble,
a flame for the bull-slayer
and shadows to dance the mystery.

In the Temple of Ceres,
I take a little yellow flower
and, half embarrassed by my silliness,
leave some money by the altar,
just small coins,
but even from the car park
I see them glint from their fist of weeds,
picked out by the sun.

Christmas 1992

No sooner is your exhaust smoke gone
than it is Christmas
and easy to be sad.
There is a choir gulping under the clock
and a man seasonally abusing his wife.
Will you shut the fuck up, he asks her,
as the Herald Angels hark.
No one is smiling anywhere,
I know because I look.
Only a shop assistant smiles –
and it is one she made up earlier –
as I pluck from a barrel of teddy bears
a last thoughtful Christmas gift.

Death on the Nith

The fans on the ceiling blur silently,
lift the hair of the brown-eyed girl
in the floral skirt drinking tea.
Through the fretwork of chair,
long legs earth on white tile.
Outside, in a blaze of sky,
two chimneys pretend to be pagodas.
Don't these children arguing the toss
chirrup like cicadas?
And isn't the breeze outside
playing through manicured gardens,
rattling through the acacia,
like a clock running slow?
No.
The man at the counter
buying a doughnut and hot Vimto
has no parallel in the east.
Soon he will read his Standard
and cough into that brown hankie
he's tugging from his coat.
He will bring the rain,
the muggy wind from the Solway,
the tinny chimes of the Midsteeple
playing Bonnie Gallowa.
He will eat his pastry next to me
and think the blood on his hands
is jam.

A Cultural Exchange in Scotland

I am walking down Irish Street,
the road that's only wide enough
for three or four lorries and a pipe band,
when I am jostled by a drunk.
He looks at my shoulder bag
of soft Cordoba leather.
"What are ye" he says, "a poof?
Fuck off!"

"Sir" I respond.
"Only a week ago I sat
in the Patio de los Naranjos
as water turned to light in Al-Andalus
and the words of Al-Bin-Asir
shone like quicksilver in my head.

Three days since,
in the ruined gardens of Medina Azzarah,
I saw the desert stretch like serenity
while the cicadas sang.

Just yesterday in La Alhambra,
the sky unrolled at my feet
round myrtle and jasmine
and the tip of heaven seemed only
a finger's span away...

and you're telling *me* to fuck off?
You fuck off!"

Pictures in the Fleshers' Arms

On a bench ringed by a picket fence
the Provost sits
beneath a telescopic hat,
his legs, like a sea-captain's,
comfortably astride,
a deed or writ clutched to a well-stuffed chest.
His collie dog,
head on the Provost's knee,
looks back at the camera
with the sharp white of its eyes,
its frozen devotion only comprehensible
when you see, on close examination,
the Provost standing on its cock.
On the right,
a man with a bonnet is limping off frame,
slowly, as you would expect
if he had great respect for the Provost,
or a long flat cock
and legal notice to quit stuffed nearby.

Also in the frame,
on top and looking used to it,
is his wife.
She is dressed sombrely,
her wide skirts merging with shadow,
the table in the foreground
metamorphosed to gloom.
There is a white hat with flaps
that reach her waist
though it seems clear she owns no anatomy,
her body having become, through constant virtue,
metaphor.
Her brows are cosh thick,
her eyes banked, deposited.
In her right hand she holds
a thick and heavily-bound book,
no prizes for guessing.

And there is a child in pantaloons.
He is being held tightly by a muscled woman,
one hand round his waist.
She is the product of some scheme
to mix the genes of Calvinists
with those of German discus-throwers
to create the perfect nanny.
The boy is suspended over the grass,
and he is staring down at the manicured lawn,
at the measure of his boundaries,
sensing the attraction of free-fall
but knowing they will never let him go.

Marking

I go along the Whitesands
every night when all the kids
have gone to bed
and with a pencil torch
and heavy-duty marker-pen
ease my way past cobblestones
and empty cans of coke
to scan the walls for – this,

here, some new work,
blistered black across the plaster,
TEACHERS ARE CRAP.
I smile.
YES INDEED THEY ARE
I write below,
TEN OUT OF TEN
YOU'RE REALLY LEARNING NOW.

Hammy and the Dog

There's an old man in the corner
with thick glasses
and a parka flecked with mud,
sitting, laurelled in smoke.
He's mouthing to a collie across the way
and though there are no words,
you know he's telling it things
about his life in Locharbriggs,
giving warnings about owners, bitches.
The dog, trapped between the legs of a yapper,
stares past the fire into Hammy's smokey eyes,
glad, for once, to be having
the loudest conversation in the room.

Kicking Anti-Clockwise

When I was young, I had this ritual.
I would kick a stone round the Dock Park,
starting at the Band-Stand.
If it went off the road
into the brittle Autumn flower beds
or the soft piles of cut grass
it cost two shots, or sometimes,
if it got lost, the game.
A proper hit
and the stone would skelp away
and disappear beyond any distinction
of path and stone
into a quiet thrill of grey
and I might just chance upon it,
in a good lie, maybe,
straight down the middle,
or trapped hopelessly
between the roots of trees.
I chose the stone before I went,
round but not too round,
and the time of day;
well before the first alsatian.
Less than twelve shots
to the bollards on the Castledykes Road
was victory:
the imaginary world in thrall
to the angles of stone and tarmac
and the skill of its champion
battling in the slow light
before the Nith was awake enough
to move towards the sea
would rejoice,
flowers would bloom in doorways,
girls beautiful beyond recall
would nod their heads as I returned,
carefully stabbing the stone homeward
to my drawer of famous stones.

If it took more than twelve
then disaster,
nightfall,
a withering.
I would skulk from the park
only hoping for another chance
and dreaming of the perfect stone,
round but not too round,
the single figure stone.
My mother would laugh at me,
put the breakfast on.
Yesterday morning,
in the drizzle on the way to work
I tried again, first time in twenty years,
for even higher stakes.
The stone was round,
not too round,
but the score was twenty three
and, as I knew,
there was no row, this time,
for having scuffed my shoes.

Tattoos

I look back through a gap
left between the fingers of trees
and the building with its wake of lights
has set sail between the clouds,
scorching them.

Here, as the road slopes into town,
there are fields behind a broken dyke,
and the grass is brittle.
Here I could stand on some hard earth,
see if in the dip beyond the lip of the hill
there is black water to soothe

but no,
just a single hedge
and the leaves as I approach
trembling on the branch.
Like my mother's hands
caught like a bird in a dazzle of cotton,
they suggest no easy rhythm
to the night.

Going Home

I'm juddering through arteries of rock.
Going home is more than geography:
it's tracing the outline of a well-loved face
with the fingers again of a child.

Water threads the scalp of hills
and soon we'll tip down to Oban
where the boats are set like buttons
on the belly of the bay
and every pavement used to lead to jam
or little fists of shingle
where you could skim a stone
all the way, it seemed, to Kerrera

and where the Columba came
bringing back the half-drowned
with their sodden duffle coats
and scarves like pennants,
home to the warm,
butting in that last mile through the Sound
while clouds closed like eyelids over stars
and a piper faint as a gull
in the roar of the night
played us home,
over all the muscles of the sea.

Ritual Roads

Checkered fields and webs of trees;
whispers of smoke and half-light
on the lochs like closing eyes.
In the crisp Sunday creases of the land
toeholds of sandstone nudge through cloud
and people, ghosts on a landscape green as sap,
move off to church on paths scattered in the hills
like scars; gingerly, as though on glass or bones
or memories, the purpose transient,
the roads, ritual.

The poet's final letter exists only in the shape of a fragment addressed to his friend Stuart 'Shug' Hanlan. The manner of its survival is, in truth, a remarkable story, adhering as it did for years to the back of an old betting slip, one of the many failed "four horse yankees" with which McMillan would squander the money he made during the 1990s tutoring the orphaned daughters of the nobility. The note is invaluable in helping the state of mind in which McMillan undertook his final fateful journey by steamer to the Stewartry.

...Mon Cher
My senses deranged by a Cold Sore,
I have left the bourgeois life of Dumfries,
with its stockbroker cottages and men with balaclavas
to live a dissipated life
among the highly-coloured shacks
and bayous of Wigtownshire.
My brother wanted me to train with Fastfoods
but I said no, I will write,
writing is my life,
I must follow the lyrical moments of my soul,
and so I am here, among the gulls.
I have taken as a mistress a half-caste bar girl,
Jean MacDougall, she is my Muse.
I write, ah how I write,
my fingers ache,
but already my opus, *The Flowers of the Machars*,
has been accepted by Ladybird...

(Here the MS ends)

Biographical Note

Born 1955. Educated for three minutes at McLaren High School till he discovered the pupils had to wear short trousers until 3rd year, Dumfries Academy and Edinburgh University. While at school he wrote over 200 versions of a poem about snow falling off a rooftop, all of them crap. Since beginning to write again in the 1980s, he has been published widely in Scotland and abroad and translated into a variety of languages. He won the Scottish National Open Poetry Competition in 1984, and was awarded SAC bursaries in 1988 and 1991. His first collection *Triumph of the Air* (Envoi Poets) was followed by *Tramontana* (Dog & Bone, 1990). In 1993 he collaborated with artist Hugh Bryden on a postcard set of poems called *Horridge* (Hugh Who? Press) which sold briskly though Bryden has, mysteriously, yet to see any cash from it.

Hugh McMillan teaches History at Dumfries Academy and has nothing but praise for Dumfries and its bohemian ways. Recently, McMillan has co-operated in the painting of murals in the local church of St Angus-in-the-Wallet, depicting local shopkeepers ascending to heaven.